THE VIETNAM WAR

"What Are We Fighting For?"

Deborah Kent

—American War Series—

ENSLOW PUBLISHERS, INC.

Bloy St. & Ramsey Ave.	P.O. Box 38
Box 777	Aldershot
Hillside, N.J. 07205	Hants GU12 6BP
U.S.A.	U.K.

> "One, two, three, what are we fighting for?
> Don't ask me I don't give a damn, next stop is Vietnam.
> Five, six, seven, open up the Pearly Gates
> Well ain't no time to wonder why,
> Whoopie, we're all going to die."
> —Sung by Country Joe McDonald, Woodstock Music and
>   Art Festival, August 15-17, 1969

Library of Congress Cataloging-in-Publication Data

Kent, Deborah.
The Vietnam war : "what are we fighting for?" / Deborah Kent.
      p. cm. — (American war series)
    Includes bibliographical references and index.
    ISBN 0-89490-527-9
    1. Vietnamese Conflict, 1961-1975—United States—Juvenile
literature. [1. Vietnamese Conflict, 1961-1975.] I. Title. II. Series.
DS558.K46 1994
959.704'3373—dc20   93-48471
                                     CIP
                                     AC

Printed in the United States of America

10 9 8 7 6 5 4 3 2 1

Illustration Credits:
Courtesy of the Prints and Photographs Division, Library of Congress, pp.
33, 75, 77; Earl McElfresh, McElfresh Map Company, pp. 14. 92; National
Archives, pp. 9, 11, 17, 21, 23, 31, 35, 37, 39, 44, 45, 51, 52, 57, 59, 61,
65, 67, 69, 71, 80, 82, 85, 87, 90, 95, 97, 101, 107, 109; National Park
Service, p. 113.

Cover Illustration:
U.S. Army Art Activity.

Contents

Foreword

On a brisk October afternoon in 1967, I marched through the streets of Washington, D.C., wearing a placard that declared, BRING THE BOYS HOME! I will never forget the thrill of gathering with thousands of others, lifting our voices in the hypnotic chant, "Peace now! Peace now!" The war in Vietnam hung over the nation like a heavy fog. I felt I was doing my tiny part to bring it to an end. Surely, our voices would be heard! At last the killing would end, and the sunshine would break through.

Like many college students during the 1960s, I was appalled by the lists of American casualties, the enemy body count, and the stories of atrocities committed by both sides. The war filled us with anger, grief, and a sense of futility. Outraged by the daily news reports, it was hard for us to grasp how the United States became involved in the conflict and why our government sent more and still more troops to faraway Southeast Asia.

Yet other Americans were distressed by the protest movement which shook the country. Though saddened by the war, they fervently believed that the United States must meet its obligations abroad. If the United States withdrew from Vietnam, it would lose respect throughout the world. Communism was a menace to world peace and freedom, and if America let Vietnam fall, other democracies might collapse as well.

A generation later, Americans are still coming to terms with the Vietnam War. With the perspective of time, it is somewhat easier to see how it all began, to examine the conflict objectively, and to seek an understanding of the outcome. The United States was directly involved in the Vietnam War for twelve years, from 1961 to 1973. But for the Vietnamese, the years of American involvement were only one chapter in a far longer struggle. It began as a fight for independence and ended in a bitter civil war that tore the country to pieces.

It has often been said that those who do not study history are condemned to repeat it. Perhaps for this reason Americans today look back to Vietnam and ask many difficult questions. By learning what occurred and why, perhaps we can work to insure that such a tragedy never happens again.

We are not about to send American boys nine or ten thousand miles from home to do what Asian boys ought to be doing for themselves.
　　　—President Lyndon B. Johnson, in a speech during his 1964 campaign for re-election.

1 Crossing the Threshold

 The Gulf of Tonkin is one of the most scenic places in all of Vietnam. Magnificent mountains rise almost straight from the sea and disappear in clouds of mist. Fishermen, in boats called junks and sampans, cast their nets among the lush green islands that fringe the shore. Yet for more than two thousand years, the Gulf of Tonkin was one of Vietnam's points of vulnerability. For the Chinese, and later the French, the gulf was the gateway to invasion of a land which seemed endlessly at war.

In 1964, the Vietnamese were fighting once again. Ten years earlier, an international agreement temporarily created two nations, North Vietnam and South Vietnam. The nations had remained separate, and now the

Communist-controlled North Vietnamese were embroiled in a fierce civil war with the non-Communist south. North Vietnam had the support of the Soviet Union and the People's Republic of China. In its struggle, South Vietnam received aid from the United States. As the fighting intensified, the North Vietnamese set up a series of radar stations along the bays and islands of the Gulf of Tonkin.

Even by the standards of tropical Vietnam, the night of August 1, 1964, was hot and humid. Aboard the destroyer U.S.S. *Maddox,* clusters of men lounged on deck, trying to catch a cooling breeze. Others had no choice but to work in the airless rooms below. They studied radar screens and searched through radio static, piecing together fragments of information. The *Maddox* was on a surveillance mission to study North Vietnamese defenses.

Suddenly, early on the morning of August 2, the crew of the *Maddox* spotted three North Vietnamese patrol boats. The *Maddox* was twenty-eight miles from the coast, still well within international waters. But the patrol boats were approaching at top speed and seemed poised to attack. As they rushed nearer, Captain John Herrick of the *Maddox* ordered his men to open fire. To this day, no one is certain which side actually fired first.

The first two torpedoes from the patrol boats missed their target, and the third was a dud which failed to explode. The *Maddox* struck back with fire from its five-inch guns. Three needle-nose crusader jets from the nearby carrier U.S.S. *Ticonderoga* sped to the *Maddox's*

One of Vietnam's most scenic locations, the Gulf of Tonkin has also historically been a gateway to invasion.

aid and strafed the patrol boats with heavy machine gun fire. The skirmish was over in twenty minutes. One patrol boat sank, and the others limped back to the safety of the coast. There were no American casualties. The *Maddox* headed south to the open sea.

Because of the thirteen-hour time difference between Vietnam and Washington, D.C., President Lyndon B. Johnson received the news on the night of August 1. At once he met with his top advisers to discuss the attack. They concluded that the North Vietnamese may have mistaken the *Maddox* for a South Vietnamese ship which bombarded two coastal islands a few days before. Johnson decided to let the incident pass without reprisal. But he ordered the *Maddox* back to the Gulf of Tonkin immediately.

Accompanied by a second destroyer, the U.S.S. *Turner Joy,* the *Maddox* returned to the Gulf of Tonkin on August 4. That night wild storms crashed over the gulf. Braced for trouble, the crewmen imagined enemy fire in each flash of lightning and crack of thunder. Suddenly, radar engineers on the destroyers saw suspicious-looking blips on their screens. The signals appeared to show an advancing enemy ship.

Wildly, both destroyers fired into darkness. There was no answering fire. No shells exploded, and no torpedoes struck. Once, the captain of the *Turner Joy* thought he saw a column of smoke towering above the waves. But when his ship drew closer, the smoke was gone. Jets from the *Ticonderoga* circled the area but found no signs of enemy vessels.

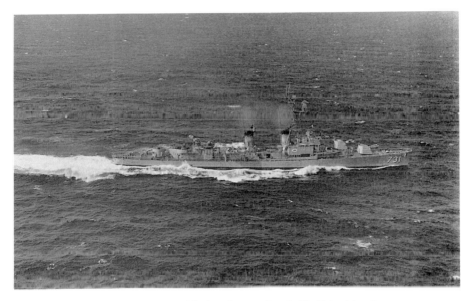

The destroyer U.S.S *Maddox* heads into the Gulf of Tonkin, August, 1964.

President Johnson was convinced that the destroyers had been attacked and determined that the United States must react swiftly. In a special televised broadcast on the night of August 4, he told the American people, "Repeated acts of violence against the armed forces of the United States must be met not only with alert defense but with a positive reply. That reply is being given as I speak to you tonight."

Near midnight, Eastern Standard Time, on August 4, 1964, American aircraft began sixty-four air sorties over four North Vietnamese patrol boat bases and a major oil storage depot. A sortie is one mission or attack by one plane. More than twenty Vietnamese vessels were destroyed. The oil depot became an inferno of roaring explosions and blazing fuel tanks. A column of smoke soared fourteen thousand feet into the air.

The second Gulf of Tonkin incident remained a mystery. In the ensuing investigations, sailors on the *Maddox* and the *Turner Joy* admitted that they had heard no enemy gunfire. No North Vietnamese boats or aircraft had been sighted. Even Captain Herrick wondered whether his ship was actually under attack. Hours after the incident he stated, "The entire action leaves many doubts, except for an apparent attempt to ambush at the beginning."[1] Karl Phaler, a communications officer on the *Turner Joy,* offered one possible explanation. "The gulf is a very funny place," he said in an interview. "You get inversion layers there that will give you very solid radar contacts that will have courses and speeds that are very trackable . . . . That may have happened to us."[2]

In the days after the incident, rumors filtered into Washington. Perhaps the second Tonkin Gulf attack had never occurred at all. In exasperation, Johnson exclaimed to one of his aides, "Those dumb stupid sailors were just shooting at flying fish!"[3]

The events that took place in the Gulf of Tonkin culminated years of mounting tension between the United States and North Vietnam. Two American presidents—Dwight D. Eisenhower and John F. Kennedy—had spent millions of dollars to aid the non-Communist South Vietnamese. By 1964, thousands of American military advisers were training and assisting the South Vietnamese army. But Johnson's decision to bomb North Vietnam carried the United States one crucial step deeper into the war—a war which proved to be the longest in the nation's history.

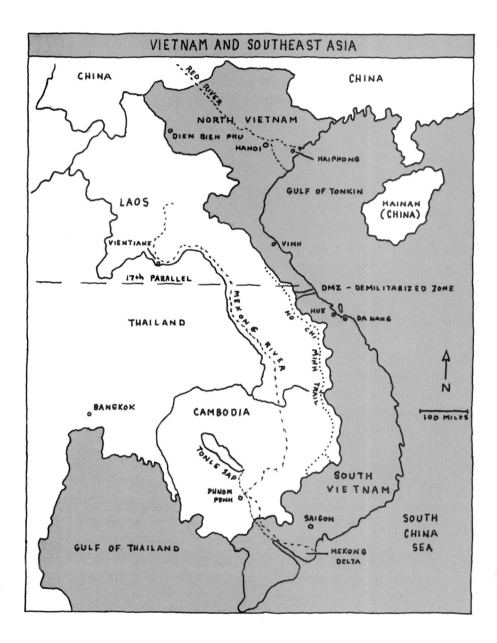

*When our soldiers are again threatened as they are today, we
will be asked for more money and more men. We will not be
able to refuse, and millions upon millions, fresh troops on
top of fresh troops, will lead to our exhaustion. Gentlemen,
we must block this route.*

—Georges Clemenceau in an address to the French Parliament
during a war to hold the French colony in Indochina, 1885.[1]

2 The Gathering Storm

 Vietnamese peasants often carry rice in
heavy baskets, one on either end of a pole
laid across their shoulders. On a map, the nation of Vietnam looks like such a pair of rice baskets, one in the
north and one in the south, connected by a mountainous
central corridor. Vietnam is about the size of the state of
California with a population during the 1960s of more
than 40 million people. Its dense tropical jungles teem
with monkeys, snakes, birds, and clouds of insects.

Vietnam curves along the eastern edge of the Indochina Peninsula, a large land mass which juts into the sea
between India and China. Three other countries also oc-
cupy the peninsula. Vietnam's immediate western
neighbors are Laos and Cambodia and west of them lies

the nation of Thailand. To the north, Vietnam borders on China. The South China Sea laps against Vietnam's eastern and southern coasts.

A Land in Turmoil

The recorded history of Vietnam stretches back to the third century B.C., when a Chinese general conquered the mountainous northern provinces. He established the independent kingdom of Nam Viet, which spread as far south as the present-day city of Hue. The Chinese later overran Nam Viet, and for a thousand years the region was under their control.

The Vietnamese adopted the Chinese form of picture writing known as calligraphy and became followers of the Chinese Buddhist and Confucian religions. But they kept their native language intact and never lost the sense that they were a distinct people. Three times Vietnam tried unsuccessfully to throw off Chinese rule.

At last, in 939 A.D., the Chinese withdrew. Through the centuries that followed, mighty Vietnamese families competed for power in a series of civil wars. From time to time, the Vietnamese also fought with the Champa people of present-day Cambodia. To the north, the Chinese were an ever-present threat.

Through all the upheavals, the Vietnamese village remained the central governing unit. No matter how many times the kingdom changed hands, each village continued to function like a tiny state with its own court system, chief, and council. As a Vietnamese proverb put

Young women of Vietnam's Ham Long District carry newly threshed rice from the fields.

it, "The laws of the emperor yield to the customs of the village."

In 1535 a Portuguese captain, Antonio da Faria, established the first European settlement in Vietnam, near today's city of Da Nang. In the years that followed, Dutch, English, and French traders found their way to Vietnam's shores. European missionaries also ventured to Indochina, winning thousands of Vietnamese converts to Catholicism. Even though the Vietnamese still fought among themselves, most shared a deep distrust of foreigners.

In the Hands of the French

During the 1860s, this distrust was confirmed when Vietnam became a colony of France. Despite continual resistance, the French hung onto Vietnam until World War II. They built roads and railroads, and brought other modern developments to the country. But French rule also imposed severe hardships on the Vietnamese people.

The French had little respect for Vietnam's ancient traditions and often treated the people with contempt. They replaced Chinese calligraphy with the western alphabet and tried to suppress the practice of Buddhism. They also grabbed land from the peasants and formed large estates under French or wealthy Vietnamese landowners. By 1914, 2 percent of the population held half the land in Vietnam. Peasants who had supported themselves by raising their own crops now labored on rice or rubber plantations run by the colonial rulers.

The French also stimulated opium trade. For centuries, people in Vietnam had smoked opium, but they used this powerful drug only in small quantities. The French developed a new, fast-burning variety of opium and opened a refinery to process it. Opium addiction soared throughout the country.

During the 1930s, Japan became increasingly hungry for more territory. In 1940, Japanese forces swept into Vietnam. The French remained, but their government was now a puppet under Japanese control.

From 1941 through 1945, Asia reeled under the onslaught of the Second World War. The tumult of warfare, combined with a series of devastating floods, led to widespread famine. More than one million Vietnamese lost their lives during this terrible period in their history.

In 1941, early in the Japanese occupation, a fifty-year-old Vietnamese man returned after thirty years of wandering abroad. He was born Nguyen Sinh Kung, the son of a traveling medicine seller. According to the many legends which sprang up around him, he had been a day laborer in Brooklyn and a pastry chef in a London hotel. In Paris he studied literature and philosophy. But he never forgot that his homeland was under foreign rule, and he was determined to help win Vietnamese independence.

During his years in Europe, he was impressed by the Communist Revolution which transformed Russia in 1917. He visited Moscow and met the Russian leaders Joseph Stalin and Leon Trotsky. Later he went to China and formed a nationalist organization among Vietnamese exiles living there.

By the time he returned to Vietnam, he had taken a new name, a name which the world would never forget. He called himself Ho Chi Minh. In Vietnamese, the name means bringer of light.

The Struggle for Independence

In Vietnam, Ho Chi Minh worked for independence with an organization called the Viet Nam Doc Lap Dong Minh, or simply, the Vietminh. American officials were wary of Ho's Communist ties. But during World War II, America was fighting against Japan, and any enemy of the Japanese seemed to be an ally.

The Japanese finally met defeat at the end of World War II in August 1945. Ho Chi Minh's National Liberation Army took over northern Vietnam. The Vietnamese emperor, Bao Dai, who had ruled as a puppet under the French and the Japanese, abdicated in favor of Ho.

On September 2, 1945, hundreds of thousands of people poured into Ba Dinh Square in the city of Hanoi. There were Buddhist monks in orange robes, peasants wearing loose-fitting black trousers and cone-shaped straw hats, and Vietminh soldiers with machetes and rifles. They had all come to see Ho Chi Minh and to hear him declare Vietnamese independence. To Americans, Ho's speech had an oddly familiar ring. "We hold the truth that all men are created equal," he told the spellbound crowd, "that they are endowed by their creator with certain unalienable rights, among them life, liberty,

Speaking to a group in 1954, Ho Chi Minh accuses the United States of interference in the struggle for Vietnamese independence.

and the pursuit of happiness."[2] In 1776, Thomas Jefferson wrote those words to the Declaration of Independence which inspired Ho Chi Minh's declaration of Vietnamese independence.

The French quickly stamped out Ho's supporters in the south, but at first they did not interfere with his government in the north. For a year it appeared that France might even accept an independent northern Vietnam as long as it maintained connections with its former rulers. But French businessmen in Vietnam wanted no part of such an arrangement. They hoped to return to the pre-war era of vast estates and total European control.

During 1946, a series of skirmishes between the French and the Vietminh finally flared into all-out war. On December 19, the French bombed the northern city of Haiphong, killing some six thousand Vietnamese soldiers and civilians. Unprepared for a large-scale confrontation, the Vietminh melted into the jungle and became guerrilla fighters. The Indochina War had begun.

Waging guerrilla warfare, small, secret military bands lived and worked in the countryside. Led by General Vo Nguyen Giap, the Vietminh harassed the French with a series of swift surprise attacks. Before the French could retaliate, the Vietminh would disappear into the mountains and jungles. As the years passed, the French poured more and more money and troops into the combat.

Meanwhile, in 1949, the Communists won the civil war in China. At the same time, relations deteriorated between the United States and Soviet Russia. Russia was

French legionnaires fight the Vietminh in the Indochina War, 1954.

America's ally against Germany during World War II. But after the war, the Soviets set up Communist governments in Poland, Czechoslovakia, Hungary, and several other countries in Eastern Europe. American leaders feared that Communism would continue to spread. The tension between the United States and the Soviet Union, which continued for more than forty years, was called the Cold War.

The Communists argued that private ownership of wealth and property led to exploitation of the working masses. Instead, they called for government control over a nation's land, factories, and natural resources. Individuals should work for the state, which would in turn provide for their needs. In theory, Communism sounded like a way to insure fair treatment for all. In practice, however, it gave the government nearly total power over people's lives.

When Communist forces from North Korea invaded democratic South Korea in 1950, thousands of American troops rushed to stop them. The Korean War raged until 1953 and ended in a stalemate. At the same time, the struggle between the French and the Vietminh aroused growing concern among American officials. Foreign policy experts feared that if one nation, however small, fell to the Communists, its neighbors could topple too, like a row of dominoes. This Domino Theory was a basic idea that fueled the Cold War.

In the early 1950s, the United States sent millions of dollars to aid France in its fight to hold Vietnam. Ho Chi Minh turned for help to Moscow and to the new

Communist government in China. Soon the struggle between the world's superpowers was being enacted in a remote land of jungles and villages, a land many Americans had never heard of before.

Dien Bien Phu and Beyond

By 1954, the French were weary of ambushes and sniper assaults. They sensed that the Vietminh might keep up their guerrilla tactics indefinitely, steadily grinding down French resistance and morale. The French were determined to lure the Vietminh into a direct confrontation. For the site of this battle, they chose their fortress at Dien Bien Phu, a village near the Laotian border in northwestern Vietnam.

Dien Bien Phu lay in a narrow valley surrounded by densely wooded hills. In December 1953, the French began to amass troops and artillery in the valley, preparing to defend it against attack. First they built an airstrip, as most of their supplies would arrive by plane and helicopter.

The Vietminh lacked air power, but they had plenty of determination and ingenuity. Thousands of soldiers set to work, carving trails through the forests. Most of these trails were too rocky and narrow for trucks or tanks. Instead the Vietminh hauled supplies on rebuilt bicycles called *xe tho*. The frame of an ordinary bicycle was reinforced, and the tires were wrapped with cloth to protect them from sharp stones. One xe tho could be loaded with four hundred pounds of supplies and pushed along the trail by several men. The Vietminh also maneuvered heavy artillery pieces through the forests. Sometimes they only moved the giant guns half a mile a day. But slowly and relentlessly, the peasant army moved the batteries into place.

The French had some fourteen thousand troops at Dien Bien Phu. On the hills above them, General Vo Nguyen Giap gathered more than forty-nine thousand men. The Vietminh also had far more artillery than the French. "We knew that a large number of artillery and gun emplacements had been prepared," wrote General Henri Navarre, commander of the French forces, "but their camouflage had been so perfect that only a small number of them had been located prior to the beginning of the attack."[3]

The fighting began near sundown on March 13, 1954. Almost immediately, the Vietminh struck the French airstrip. Vietminh artillery barrages left it so pitted with shell craters that planes could no longer land with supplies and reinforcements. For the rest of the battle, the French could only drop food and ammunition into the valley by parachute. Often these supplies fell on Vietminh territory and were captured by the enemy.

The battle for Dien Bien Phu dragged on for nearly two months. Both sides suffered horrifying casualties. When the yearly monsoon struck in April, the soldiers struggled through deep, sucking mud and sometimes stood in water up to their waists. Neither side had enough doctors or medicines. As many men perished of wounds as died on the battlefield.

Slowly, day by day, the Vietminh pushed nearer,

driving the French into a smaller and smaller area at the middle of the valley. But the cruel losses from French shells were eroding Vietminh morale. Years later, Giap admitted, "At that time a negative tendency appeared among our officers and men under various forms: fear of casualties, losses, fatigue, difficulties and hardships; underestimation of the enemy; . . . self-defeat."[4]

The world watched as the French clung to Dien Bien Phu, fighting on against hopeless odds. At last, on May 6, the Vietminh rushed in for a final, deadly assault. The following day, the French raised the flag of surrender.

Meanwhile, an international conference had convened in Geneva, Switzerland, to work out the terms of peace between France and the Vietminh. In addition to delegates from France and the Vietnamese Communists, there were representatives of the French-sponsored government which controlled parts of southern Vietnam. Diplomats also came from China, Great Britain, the Soviet Union, and the United States—all nations with a stake in Vietnam's future.

After strenuous debate, the conference temporarily divided Vietnam at the 17th parallel—that is, 17 degrees north latitude on the map. Years later the strip of land along the 17th parallel came to be known as the demilitarized zone or DMZ. Under the Geneva Agreement, the French would withdraw from North Vietnam, which would be governed by the Vietminh. The Vietminh and the French would both leave South Vietnam. The agreement also called for an election to be held in 1956. This election would decide what government should rule a reunited Vietnam.

Neither the United States nor South Vietnam signed the final peace agreement. Both feared that a nationwide election so soon after the war would be a sweeping victory for Ho Chi Minh and the Vietminh. In the south as well as in the north, Ho Chi Minh was immensely popular. Like America's George Washington, Ho was seen as a dedicated revolutionary leader who had freed his country from foreign rule. But, U.S. officials wondered, if Ho and the Communists controlled all of Vietnam, which domino would be next to fall?

I swear to fight to my last breath
To erase from the land of the south
Even the shadow of a foreign soldier,
To bring bread, peace, liberty
Over the entire sweep of my sacred motherland,
To give a worthy account of a fighter
Of the Liberation Army of South Vietnam.

—Lien Nam, a poet of the National Liberation Front[1]

3 Down the Slippery Slope

 The months after the peace agreement saw a mass migration from North Vietnam to the south. Fearing reprisal by the Communists, nearly one million North Vietnamese citizens left their homes to settle in South Vietnam. Most of the refugees were Roman Catholics. South Vietnamese Prime Minister Ngo Dinh Diem, elected in 1955, encouraged this exodus with the slogan, "God has gone south."

Ho Chi Minh still had the sweeping support of the majority of people in both North and South Vietnam. Ho seemed to be a true man of the people. Even at public appearances he was barefoot and dressed in the loose black trousers of a peasant. People affectionately called

him Uncle Ho, as though he were a kindly relative looking after his family.

In contrast, Prime Minister Diem seemed arrogant
and remote. In a predominantly Buddhist nation, he was
a devout Catholic who had once considered becoming a
priest. Diem disliked publicity and grew increasingly re-
clusive as the years passed. Although he was personally
honest, he was surrounded by corrupt officials who ex-
ploited the people to gain wealth and power.

To stifle opposition, Diem turned for help to the Secret Police, headed by his brother, Ngo Dinh Nhu. Nhu
arrested anyone who had fought against the French or
expressed sympathy for Ho's regime. Some people were
sent to prison simply because they still had relatives in
the north. Many of the prisoners were tortured, and
their property was confiscated by corrupt officials.

Meanwhile, Ho Chi Minh launched a purge in the
north. Ho and his followers were determined to take
land from the wealthy for redistribution among the peasants. Communist Party spokesmen and spokeswomen
known as cadres fanned out through the villages, arrest-
ing alleged landowners and throwing them into prison.
Many of the people taken into custody had never controlled vast estates, but had only small holdings of three
or four acres. Sometimes villagers pointed out someone
to the cadres and accused him or her of loyalty to the
French. Thousands of suspects were taken into custody
on no more evidence than a neighbor's pointing finger.

The year 1956 came and went, and the national

South Vietnamese Prime Minister Ngo Dinh Diem addresses the
Civil Guard in 1955.

election was never held. The French had left Vietnam, yet war dragged on. Now, however, Vietnamese were fighting Vietnamese.

Ho Chi Minh still dreamed of a united Vietnam. If he could strengthen his southern following, he hoped eventually to overthrow Diem's government and bring the two Vietnams together under Communist rule. Beginning in 1959, cadres and soldiers from the north rallied villagers in South Vietnam's Mekong River delta to Ho Chi Minh's cause. Disparagingly, Diem referred to them as Vietcong—Vietnamese Communists. The Communists called themselves the National Liberation Front (NLF).

The Ho Chi Minh Trail

For centuries, merchants from China had carried goods along a network of jungle trails through Laos and Cambodia into southern Vietnam. Now North Vietnamese soldiers wound their way along these same paths, carrying weapons and other supplies. This twisting, half-hidden route through the undergrowth came to be called the Ho Chi Minh Trail.

The Ho Chi Minh Trail boasted every hardship the jungle could offer. Giant, blood-sucking leeches lurked in the streams. Stinging insects and malaria-carrying mosquitoes swarmed around the travelers night and day. During the heavy rains of the monsoon seasons, the paths became sloughs of mud.

For a soldier on foot or pushing a bicycle, the trip from North Vietnam to the Mekong Delta could take as

Ho Chi Minh with some of his family.

long as three months. "We walked eleven hours a day, and the more we walked, the more bored and morose we became," one Vietcong soldier recalled later. "There were many things I missed. . . . I wanted badly to see my mother, to be close to her. And then what I wanted badly was a whole day of rest."[2] Year after year, a steady stream of soldiers endured the sickness, hunger, fear, and exhaustion for Uncle Ho.

The Enemy of My Enemy

"The enemy of my enemy is my friend." This old saying sums up President Dwight D. Eisenhower's attitude toward Prime Minister Ngo Dinh Diem. Diem was not an ideal leader, but Eisenhower knew that at least he opposed the Communists. For this reason, Eisenhower determined to give Diem America's support. Eventually, he hoped, a stronger leader would emerge, and South Vietnam could survive on its own. For now, Diem and South Vietnam needed America's help in the fight against Communism.

Eisenhower did not send combat troops, but he did send some seven hundred military advisers to help the South Vietnamese plan and carry out their campaign. He also poured American money into Vietnam, just as he had during the Indochina War between the French and the Vietminh.

On the evening of July 8, 1959, six American advisers were watching a movie at their base near Bien Hoa, twenty miles northeast of Saigon, the South Vietnamese capital. Just as one of the men switched on the lights to

Dwight D. Eisenhower speaks with Barry Goldwater in 1964. During his presidency, Eisenhower poured money into South Vietnam and sent 700 military advisers.

change a reel of film, a band of Communist guerrillas thrust machine guns through the open windows. The room exploded in screams and the deadly rattle of automatic fire. The incident was over in minutes. Five people lay dead—two South Vietnamese guards, an eight-year-old Vietnamese boy, and two of the American advisers. They were Major Dale R. Buis and Master Sergeant Chester M. Ovnand. Buis and Ovnand were the first Americans to die in the conflict which came to be known as the Vietnam War.

In 1961, a new president took office in the United States. John F. Kennedy was youthful, handsome, and vigorous. In his inaugural address, he promised, "We shall pay any price, bear any burden, meet any hardship, support any friend, oppose any foe to assure the survival of liberty." Like Eisenhower, Kennedy firmly believed in the Domino Theory. He did not want to deepen America's involvement in Vietnam, but he feared the consequences of a Communist takeover. A few top officials counseled him to withdraw from Vietnam altogether. But Kennedy was convinced that America would lose international prestige if it abandoned Eisenhower's commitment to South Vietnam.

In 1961, Kennedy sent General Maxwell Taylor to survey the situation in Vietnam. Taylor recommended that the United States send combat troops to prop up Diem's regime. Kennedy was reluctant to send in a fighting force. But by early in 1962, he had increased the American military presence in Vietnam from seven

South Vietnamese troops in combat with the Vietcong, 1961.

hundred military advisers to more than four thousand. He also sent three hundred helicopters for use by the South Vietnamese army.

At first, the Vietcong were terrified by the helicopters. Most Vietcong were simple peasants who had never before encountered these fantastic machines that roared above the treetops and hailed machine-gun bullets. In panic they fled from their jungle hiding places only to become easy targets on open ground. The Army of the Republic of Vietnam (known as ARVN, pronounced Arvin) raided Communist strongholds through the spring and summer of 1962. Its morale soared with one triumph after another.

Soon, however, the Vietcong adapted to the air assaults. They protected themselves by digging trenches and underground tunnels. They also obtained more powerful guns which could shoot the helicopters out of the sky. Then, in January 1963, a battalion of Vietcong stood its ground against a large, well-armed South Vietnamese force near the village of Ap Bac. South Vietnamese morale crumbled. The ARVN grew cautious, reluctant to lose more men and equipment.

In the meantime, Diem and his brother Nhu had launched a fresh program to curb the spread of Communism. To defend the South Vietnamese people from Communist infiltrators, they moved whole villages to strategic hamlets. By the end of 1962, some 34 percent of all South Vietnamese villagers had been resettled. The strategic hamlets were large enclosures, surrounded by moats and fences of sharpened bamboo stakes. To the

Manned by ARVN troops, helicopters approach an enemy target.

villagers, uprooted and confused, the hamlets seemed more like prisons than shelters.

Unknown to the ARVN, many of the villagers herded into the strategic hamlets actually belonged to the Vietcong. Inside the stockades they went on talking to the peasants about Ho Chi Minh and his Communist ideals. Torn from their homes, their rice fields, and the graves of their ancestors, the peasants listened more closely than ever. The strategic hamlets proved to be one of the strongest weapons against the government of Ngo Dinh Diem.

The Fall of Diem

During 1962 and 1963, Ngo Dinh Diem and his brother Nhu grew steadily more unpopular with the South Vietnamese people. Diem lived in fear of an uprising and withdrew from the public view. More and more power rested with Nhu and his wife, known to the world as Madame Nhu. Madame Nhu quickly earned the nickname the "Dragon Lady" after a sinister comic strip character.

Nhu and Madame Nhu imposed a series of repressive laws that stifled Vietnamese society. They made dancing and popular music illegal and forbade women to wear make-up or western-style skirts. They shut down bars and gambling houses. They required government approval for all public gatherings, including weddings and funerals. To enforce these regulations, Nhu had the backing of the Secret Police.

Despite the laws against public gatherings, thousands

of people poured into the streets of the city of Hue on May 7, 1963, for the annual celebration of Buddha's birthday. Defying a ban on all flags except that of the national government, the crowd raised dozens of traditional Buddhist banners. Suddenly five armored cars pulled up, and government police ordered the crowd to disperse. As people began to scatter, the police opened fire. In the panic that followed, a woman and eight children were trampled to death.

The incident at Hue highlighted the ongoing tension between the Buddhist majority and the Catholic-controlled government. Over the next few weeks, Buddhists organized rallies and hunger strikes to protest their oppression under Diem. But no one in the government seemed to notice.

On June 11, an elderly Buddhist monk named Thich Quang Duc sat down at a busy Saigon intersection and doused his orange robes with gasoline. Then, before a horrified crowd, he calmly set himself ablaze. Reporters had been advised of his intentions and captured the scene on film. The ghastly image flashed across television screens around the world.

Half a dozen more Buddhist monks and nuns committed suicide by burning, called immolation, over the ensuing weeks. Their protest shocked the world, but Diem and his family remained indifferent. "Let them burn and we shall clap our hands," Madame Nhu told a reporter.[3] On another occasion, Madame Nhu declared, "If the Buddhists want to have another barbecue, I will be glad to supply the gasoline."[4]

On August 21, Nhu's Secret Police launched a series of raids on Buddhist temples in Hue, Saigon, and other cities throughout South Vietnam. More than fourteen hundred people were arrested, and many of them were tortured. At last the Kennedy administration realized that the United States could no longer support the Diem regime. There would have to be a change if there was any hope for a democracy.

The next day, Henry Cabot Lodge arrived in Saigon to serve as the new U.S. Ambassador to South Vietnam. Lodge had extensive experience in foreign policy, including seven years as America's chief delegate to the United Nations. Within a week he cabled Kennedy, "We are launched on a course from which there is no respectable turning back, the overthrow of the Diem government. . . . There is no turning back because there is no possibility in my view that the war can be won under a Diem administration."[5] Kennedy gave Lodge tacit authority to act in whatever way he saw fit.

Several ARVN generals had expressed growing dissatisfaction with the Diem regime. Now the United States stood by as they plotted the prime minister's overthrow. The coup came on November 1, 1963. Three generals seized control of the National Palace. But Diem and Nhu fled through a secret tunnel and hid in Cholon, Saigon's Chinese quarter. At a Catholic church in Cholon they made confession and took Holy Communion. Then they hid in the home of a friend and waited.

Through the long afternoon and evening the brothers sat helplessly. Perhaps they noted that the date was

November 1, All Soul's Day in the Catholic calendar. In many parts of the world, November 1 is a day for remembering the dead.

The following morning, the brothers were discovered in their hiding place. South Vietnamese officers escorted them to the back of an armored vehicle, where they were both shot to death. Crowds cheered as the armored car rolled through the streets, the corpses of hated leaders sprawled across the hood.

Kennedy and Lodge had thought Diem and Nhu would simply be forced to leave the country. They had not expected that the brothers would die in the coup. Still, they believed that Diem's overthrow would permit a stronger leader to emerge, a leader worthy of American support. Lodge congratulated the insurgent generals on a job well done. In a spirit of optimism he cabled Kennedy, "The prospects now are for a shorter war."

Send in the Marines!

Three weeks after the murder of Diem and Nhu, on November 22, 1963, an assassin gunned down President John F. Kennedy in Dallas, Texas. The tragedy thrust Vice President Lyndon B. Johnson into the presidency. That night, top officials spent hours briefing Johnson on crucial matters which faced the nation. Vietnam was scarcely mentioned. As one aide later remarked, "Vietnam at that time was a cloud no bigger than a man's fist on the horizon. We hardly discussed it because it wasn't worth discussing."[6]

Kennedy and Lodge had hoped that Diem's removal

A firm believer in the Domino Theory, President John F. Kennedy increased American military presence in South Vietnam.

The first U.S. Marines land at Da Nang in South Vietnam in March, 1965.

would stabilize South Vietnam. But over the next twenty months, generals grabbed power from one another in a bewildering series of coups. In the meantime, the North Vietnamese gathered strength for a long, drawn-out war. Early in 1964, construction crews began work on the Ho Chi Minh Trail, widening it to handle heavy vehicles. Beneath the jungles, the North Vietnamese dug a labyrinth of underground barracks, storerooms, fuel depots, and hospitals.

In March 1964, President Johnson appointed retired army general Maxwell Taylor to serve as American Ambassador to South Vietnam, and he put General William Westmoreland in command of the U.S. military advisory forces. He also sent teams of doctors, teachers, and agricultural specialists. By setting up hospitals and schools, by teaching the peasants better ways to raise pigs and chickens, the U.S. hoped to win the hearts and minds of the South Vietnamese people.

Gradually Johnson realized that the situation in Vietnam was far worse than he had imagined. North Vietnam was receiving more help from the Soviet Union, installing radar stations around cities and along the coast. Johnson authorized American destroyers to cruise the Tonkin Gulf on survey missions. Tensions led to the Gulf of Tonkin incident which in turn triggered the first American bombing raids on North Vietnamese territory.

"We seek no wider war," Johnson told the American public again and again. He was deeply committed to a set of new domestic programs at home and was reluctant to expend more resources in Vietnam. But like Kennedy, he feared the loss of American prestige if the United States should abandon the war effort.

In the heat of excitement after the incidents in the Gulf of Tonkin, Congress passed a groundbreaking resolution on August 7, 1964. The Gulf of Tonkin Resolution authorized the president to take "all necessary measures to repel attacks against U.S. forces and to prevent further aggression." It gave the president the power to carry on the conflict in Vietnam as he saw fit, without a formal declaration of war. As Johnson remarked, the resolution "was like Grandma's night-dress—it covered everything."[7]

The Vietcong were growing more aggressive. In November 1964, they attacked the American base at Bien Hoa, destroying five B-57 jets and damaging twenty more. Within weeks they attacked the Catholic village of Binh Jia, fifty miles south of Saigon. Then, on Christmas Eve, a bomb exploded in the Brinks Hotel in Saigon. Two American officers died, and fifty-eight were injured. Not even the heart of Saigon was safe.

On February 7, 1965, the Vietcong struck at the American fort near the town of Pleiku in the mountains of northern South Vietnam. Within hours American jets rained bombs on the North Vietnamese camp at Dong Hoi. Soon after these retaliatory strikes were over, the United States launched a massive series of air strikes called Operation Rolling Thunder. Rolling Thunder would pound North Vietnam with bombs for the next three years.

On February 22, General Westmoreland asked for

two battalions of U.S. Marines to defend the American base at Da Nang. The Marines hit the beach on March 8, 1965, dressed in full uniform, ready to do battle. They were the first American combat troops to set foot in Asia since the Korean War.

The Marine landing received little coverage from the news media. Nearly everyone expected them home in only a few weeks. But the landing of the Marines was a decisive step, carrying the United States deeper into its longest war.

We will continue to fight as long as
necessary—ten, fifteen, twenty, fifty years.
—North Vietnamese Commander Vo Nguyen Giap, 1969.[1]

4   War Without End

After the first U.S. Marines landed at Da Nang in March 1965, more American troops poured into Vietnam each week. By December, the number had swelled to two hundred thousand. A year later that number had doubled, reaching four hundred thousand. In the United States, the news media referred to this heightened American involvement as escalation.

Relying on its advanced military technology, the United States planned an offensive campaign of heavy bombing from immense B-52 jets. In addition, a relentless series of search and destroy missions would rout out Vietcong from the jungles and villages of South Vietnam. The Communists countered defensively, avoiding direct confrontations wherever possible. Instead, they depended on the guerrilla tactics which had been so effective against the French. They attempted to wear down their enemies with lightning-swift surprise attacks.

Beginning in March 1965, giant eight-engine B-52 bombers dumped tons of explosives on North Vietnam. Fighter bombers, operating in coordination with ground troops, dropped napalm bombs on enemy positions. Napalm was a jelly-like substance made from petroleum. It was dropped in cannisters which shattered when they hit the ground. As soon as it was exposed to the air, the napalm burst into fierce, scorching flames. In June 1965, the United States made forty-eight hundred attacks on North Vietnamese targets. By early 1967, American planes flew twelve thousand bombing missions per month. During Operation Rolling Thunder, the United States dropped more bombs on North Vietnam than it had on Europe during all of World War II.

American military leaders hoped the bombing raids would destroy North Vietnam's factories and supply routes and would kill so many people that the enemy would surrender in despair. But North Vietnam was not dependent on factories, and supply routes were hard to strike as they twisted through the jungle. The North Vietnamese had few tanks, little artillery, and virtually no aircraft so they did not need spare parts or fuel. The bombing raids did little to interfere with the type of warfare they waged.

Nevertheless, the air strikes were terrifying, and they killed tens of thousands of people. A sixteen-year-old

Two B-52's drop bombs on a Vietcong stronghold in the jungles of
South Vietnam.

Flanked by four F-105 Thunder Chief fighter bombers, an American B-66 drops bombs in Vietcong strongholds in South Vietnam.

North Vietnamese nurse described her journey to a hospital in Laos:

> The Americans had denuded the jungles with their bombing, and there was no place to hide. They would light up the area with flares and drop bombs everywhere. Each time they flew overhead, our commander ordered us to disperse and dig foxholes. But the bombs fell close, and I shook with fear. . . . Even after the bombing had stopped, I couldn't focus my eyes, and my head ached for hours.[2]

Despite the ferocious bombing, North Vietnamese soldiers were at home in the mountains and jungles, surviving on rice and sleeping on the ground. They needed none of the luxuries which American troops considered essential—waterproof tents, insect repellent, and chocolate bars. Though they faced the constant terror of assaults from the air, they went on fighting.

Escalation

America flung itself into the war with everything money and modern technology could provide. Soldiers carried fully automatic M-16 rifles. Transport planes were armed with machine guns that fired eighteen thousand rounds per minute. The air swarmed with helicopters, fighter planes, and huge B-52 bombers. Destroyers, tankers, and patrol boats cruised along the coast, and lighter craft threaded the rivers and canals of the Mekong Delta. In addition, there were vast quantities of medicines and surgical equipment, canned and packaged foods, boots, jungle fatigues, toothpaste, and shaving kits. The Americans even provided movie projectors, air conditioners, tape decks, and live entertainers to boost their men's morale. By 1967, the United States was shipping an average of one hundred pounds of supplies per day for every soldier stationed in Vietnam.

America's commitment to the war transformed South Vietnam almost overnight. In 1965, the land was a patchwork of villages and rice paddies. Barefoot peasants plowed the fields with the help of water buffaloes. Saigon, the capital, looked like a town in southern France, with walled gardens, shaded verandas, and friendly sidewalk cafes.

Then, almost without warning, bulldozers gouged out great roads for trucks and armored personnel carriers. They leveled huge airstrips near the American bases at Da Nang and Bien Hoa. Bridges were built across the Mekong River and its maze of tributaries. Enormous dredges turned the sleepy fishing port at Cam Ranh Bay into deep harbors for mighty U.S. warships.

Saigon adapted quickly to the flood of American soldiers with money in their pockets. Rowdy saloons replaced cafes. Beggars and prostitutes thronged the sidewalks. With so much money pouring into the city, corruption flourished. Canned goods, phonograph records, typewriters, and wristwatches had a way of vanishing from army warehouses, only to reappear for sale on Saigon street corners.

In June 1965, Air Vice Marshal Nguyen Cao Ky became South Vietnam's prime minister, ending the unrest that began with Diem's assassination. At thirty-four, Ky

Comedian Bob Hope and dancers Harold and Fayard Nicholas entertain troops aboard the U.S.S. *Ticonderoga* in December, 1965.

was a hero of the ARVN air corps. He was a colorful figure who usually wore a pearl-handled pistol in his belt. Ambassador Maxwell Taylor believed that Ky would develop the stable government which South Vietnam so badly needed. But the people of South Vietnam distrusted Ky. He was too young, too flamboyant, and too close to the Americans. Ky remained in power until 1967, when he was succeeded by his former vice-minister, Nguyen Van Thieu. Thieu served for eight years, until April 1975. During most of that period, Ky held the position of vice-minister under Thieu.

Serving in Country

"When I stepped off the plane at Tan Son Nhut [Saigon Airport], the heat that was coming from the ground hit me in the face," recalled Richard J. Ford III of the 25th Army Division. "The odor from the climate was so strong, it hit me and I said, 'God damn! Where am I? What is this?' "[3]

To the thousands of American soldiers and Marines who arrived "in country," Vietnam was as incomprehensible as the complex language of its people. Most Americans came from cities or suburbs; most Vietnamese people had grown up in small villages. Most Americans were Catholic, Protestant, or Jewish; the Vietnamese were overwhelmingly Buddhist. The Americans had traveled thousands of miles to fight a war whose origins they scarcely understood. The Vietnamese were fighting on their own soil, for their homes, their families, and their future.

After disembarking at Saigon Harbor, an American tank rolls through the streets of South Vietnam's capital city.

After basic training in the United States, army recruits served a twelve-month "hitch" in "Nam." Only about ten percent of these soldiers ever saw combat. Most were part of the military's vast support staff, serving as mechanics, medics, bookkeepers, or quartermasters in charge of supplies. Even the combat troops experienced long stretches of inactivity. "This war is so frustrating and boring at times that it would try the Pope's patience," Lieutenant Desmond Barry of the 7th Regiment, First Marine Division, wrote to his family. "It is made up with extended periods of boredom interspersed with periods of utter mayhem."[4]

Few conventional battles were fought during the Vietnam War. Rarely did large opposing forces meet face to face to fight for a crucial piece of territory. Instead, the ARVN and American forces carried out search and destroy missions against the Vietcong. Helicopters delivered them to areas where Vietcong were suspected to hide. The soldiers combed the jungles, questioned villagers, and killed as many Vietcong as they could. After a given number of days or weeks, returning helicopters carried them back to their base.

The search and destroy missions embodied all the fear and horror of the war. Men stepped on exploding land mines which tore their bodies to pieces. Sometimes they were ambushed by Vietcong soldiers who lay concealed in the dense jungle foliage. "We got fire fights after fire fights, my first taste of death," said Robert Rawls, a rifleman with the First Cavalry Division. "After fire fights you could smell it. They brought the guys

American soldiers on patrol faced the risks of stepping on exploding land mines and being ambushed by Vietcong soldiers concealed in the dense jungles.

back wrapped up in ponchos. . . . They just threw them up on the helicopter and put all these empty supplies on top of them. . . . I can still see those guys. . . . I said, 'What are we over here fighting for?' "[5]

The men in a patrol squad grew intensely close to one another on these marches through the jungle. They fought heroically to save their buddies, men who would die for them if the need arose. Survival became all important. If a man could stay alive until his hitch was over, he could go home. Beyond that, nothing seemed to matter.

In this form of warfare, no territory was gained. Yet U.S. officials assured the American people that the war was being won, based on the enemy body count. However, the body count could be wildly misleading. "If we killed seven, by the time we got back to base camp it would have gotten to twenty-eight," recalled Army Specialist Harold Bryant. "Then by the time it got down to Westmoreland's office in Saigon it went up to fifty-four. And by the time it left from Saigon and went to Washington, it went up to a hundred twenty-five. To prove we were really out there doing our job, doing really more than we were doing."[6]

Many of the American troops came to Vietnam eager to serve their country. They believed they were fighting to save South Vietnam from Communism. But often the ARVN soldiers fled from combat, letting the Americans do the fighting for them. They hardly seemed to care whether South Vietnam won the war or not.

To complicate matters further, the Americans could

In 1966, President Lyndon B. Johnson visits U.S. troops stationed in Vietnam.

not easily distinguish friendly South Vietnamese villagers from Vietcong. Sometimes innocent-looking old women or children as young as twelve proved to be carrying hand grenades. At other times, American soldiers shot people they believed to be Vietcong and discovered too late that they were tragically mistaken. It was all hopelessly confusing—the language, the minds of the people, the meaning of a war which dragged on and on with no end in sight.

The Tet Offensive

By 1968, war was a way of life in Vietnam. It had acquired its own traditions and unspoken rules. One of these traditions was an unofficial cease-fire during the three-day celebration of Tet, the lunar new year.

Tet is the most important holiday in Vietnam. It is a joyful celebration and a solemn rite of passage, a time of forgiveness and hope. Far-flung relatives return home, and children receive presents. No one goes to work. People crowd the streets to watch processions and fireworks displays. Tet is like an exuberant blend of Christmas, Easter, and the Fourth of July.

As Tet approached in 1968, the Americans were not in a festive mood. For nearly six weeks, Vietcong and North Vietnamese regular forces had besieged the Marine garrison at Khe Sanh near the Laotian border. At last the Americans and South Vietnamese had the chance to confront the enemy in a conventional battle, with numbers and technology on their side. General Westmoreland and President Johnson focused their attention on Khe Sanh and were determined to score a military victory.

At 2:45 A.M. on the morning of January 31, 1968, the opening day of Tet, an explosion ripped through the American Embassy in Saigon. Through the gaping hole in the concrete wall, a band of nineteen Vietcong rushed into the courtyard. They threw themselves upon the inner door, but it would not yield. For six hours, the Vietcong crouched behind benches and flowerpots in the courtyard, exchanging fire with the military police who defended the embassy. At last, by 9 A.M., all of the assailants lay dead or wounded.

The bold assault on the American embassy was one of some hundred surprise attacks on cities, villages, and military outposts all over South Vietnam. More than seventy thousand Vietcong and North Vietnamese soldiers took part in the campaign, which came to be known as the Tet Offensive. The attacks had been carefully planned for three months. While the ARVN and American forces were distracted by the fighting at Khe Sanh, the Vietcong had quietly smuggled arms into Saigon, Da Nang, and other cities. They concealed guns and explosives in truckloads of rice and even staged mock funerals, hiding weapons in the coffins. One Vietcong spy worked as a chauffeur at the American Embassy.

Mercilessly, the attackers targeted foreigners, South Vietnamese officials, and their families. The Americans and the ARVN fought back furiously. Again and again, the Vietcong and North Vietnamese gained ground, only to be killed or driven away.

The most brutal fighting of those terrible days took place in the majestic ancient city of Hue. Some seventy-five hundred Communist troops poured into the city, hoisting the gold-starred flag of the National Liberation Front over the Citadel, Hue's imperial palace. Cadres searched from house to house, dragging out merchants, teachers, minor officials—anyone remotely sympathetic with the Americans and the South Vietnamese government. Thousands were executed, many after days of torture. Some three thousand bodies were buried along nearby riverbanks and in jungle clearings.

For more than three weeks, three U.S. Marine and eleven ARVN battalions fought to liberate Hue from the Communists. Armored tanks rumbled through the streets, bombarding buildings which might harbor North Vietnamese soldiers. Dodging Communist snipers who crouched on roofs and balconies, Marines and ARVN troops spattered houses with machine-gun fire. Slowly, painfully, they regained building after building, street after street.

One Marine lieutenant remembered trying to rescue a platoon which had been ambushed by the enemy. "Somebody threw an unconscious [man] on the back of a tank. Suddenly, an enemy rocket struck the turret, pieces of shrapnel hitting the Marine. The guy came tumbling off the tank, rudely awakened. His foot was gone."

On February 24, General Westmoreland announced that Hue had been recaptured at last. Some ten thousand Vietnamese civilians had lost their lives in the battle,

Saigon under attack by the Vietcong during the 1968 Tet Offensive.

many the victims of random U.S. and ARVN fire. Another hundred thousand people were homeless. At least half of Hue's buildings were in ruins. One eyewitness reported that the once magnificent city was now "a shattered, stinking hulk, its streets choked with rubble and rotting bodies."[7]

The Communists suffered devastating losses by the time the Tet Offensive was over. Some officials estimated that as many as forty thousand Communist soldiers were killed or wounded. "The well-laid plans of the North Vietnamese and Vietcong have failed," reported General Westmoreland. "The enemy exposed himself by virtue of his strategy, and suffered heavy casualties."[8]

From a military standpoint, Westmoreland was correct, the Tet Offensive was a failure. Yet, the American public reacted to the Tet Offensive with shock and horror. TV cameramen showed the Embassy under attack and captured Saigon's chief of police as he shot a bound, helpless Vietcong prisoner in the head. Newsmen wondered aloud how the enemy's massive plans had gone undetected. Perhaps the government had been deceiving the public all along with its reports that the United States was winning the war.

For many Americans, the Tet Offensive was a crisis of trust. It crystallized the nation's growing doubts about the wisdom of fighting in Vietnam and the government's conduct in the war. Many people still believed that the United States must not relent in its efforts to stop the spread of Communism. But a growing chorus of voices

Fleeing the Tet Offensive fighting in Hue, Vietnamese civilians manage to cross the Perfume River despite a bombed bridge.

called for withdrawal from the Vietnam struggle, demanding peace at any price.

The Communists lost tens of thousands in the Tet Offensive, but they scored a sweeping psychological victory.

The Changing of the Guard

In February 1968, CBS news anchor Walter Cronkite visited Vietnam. After talking with soldiers, officers, and Vietnamese civilians, he returned to the United States with a grim report. On the evening news of February 27 he stated, "It seems more certain than ever that the bloody experience of Vietnam is to end in a stalemate."

When Congress passed the Tonkin Resolution in 1964, 85 percent of the American people approved of President Johnson's actions in Vietnam. But as the United States sank deeper into the war, public confidence waned. Even some of Johnson's top officials began to raise serious questions about America's involvement in Southeast Asia. In 1966 National Security Advisor McGeorge Bundy and Under-Secretary of State George Ball resigned after raising doubts about American's policy in Vietnam. In 1967 Senator J. William Fulbright led Senate hearings on the war.

By the close of 1967, more than half of all Americans felt that the nation had made a grave mistake by entering the Vietnam conflict. But these critics were severely divided over what should be done. Some said all American troops should get out of Vietnam. Others believed that the United States should redouble its efforts and defeat

President Johnson discusses the situation in Vietnam with General Westmoreland, April, 1968.

the Communists at any cost, even it if meant the use of nuclear weapons.

Urged on by General Westmoreland and the Pentagon, President Johnson steadily escalated the war from the time he took office in 1963. He was haunted by the fear that he might go down in history as the first American president ever to lose a war. He was hurt and saddened by his growing unpopularity. He once told a press secretary, "I feel like a hitchhiker caught in a hailstorm on a Texas highway. I can't run, I can't hide, and I can't make it stop."[9]

In 1968, Johnson was up for reelection. But two other candidates challenged him for the Democratic nomination. Campaigning on a peace platform, Minnesota Senator Eugene McCarthy nearly won the New Hampshire primary early in March. An even stronger opponent was Senator Robert Kennedy, brother of the assassinated president, John F. Kennedy.

On March 25, Johnson called a meeting of the "wise men," a group of thirteen of the nation's most respected present and former leaders. Among them were McGeorge Bundy, Henry Cabot Lodge, George Ball, and Maxwell Taylor. Almost without exception, the "wise men" warned Johnson that America was embroiled in a war it could not hope to win.

Six days later, on March 31, Johnson addressed the nation in a televised speech. He began by announcing that he would decrease the bombing raids over North Vietnam and would try to open peace negotiations. Then he concluded, "I shall not seek and I will not

Army Vice Chief of Staff Creighton Abrams and General William Westmoreland with members of their staffs at Saigon's Ton Son Nhut Airport.

accept the nomination of my party for another term as your president."

Johnson's announcement took the public completely by surprise. Antiwar protesters celebrated, convinced that their efforts had made a difference. All over the country, people asked each other who the next president would be and what he would do about the war.

In June 1968, Robert Kennedy was killed by an assassin as he campaigned in Los Angeles. At the Democratic Convention in August, antiwar protesters clashed with Chicago police, and hundreds of people were arrested. The nation was shocked by TV images of young men and women being clubbed by police in the streets. The Democrats nominated Vice-President Hubert Humphrey. But the election in November went to the Republican candidate, Richard M. Nixon.

In 1954, when he served as vice president under Eisenhower, Nixon had urged the United States to send troops to aid the French in their struggle against the Vietminh. He was uncompromising in his stand against Communism and believed that the White House should hold the reins of power in national government. Nixon won the election with his campaign promise to bring about "peace with honor."

Where have all the soldiers gone?
Gone to graveyards every one—
When will they ever learn?
Oh, when will they ever learn?
　　　　　　　—Protest ballad by folksinger Pete Seeger

5 Beyond the Battlefield

In 1966, a popular American song celebrated the heroism of the Green Berets, a specially trained army unit which fought in the jungles of Vietnam. At that time, most Americans who gave the matter any thought supported the nation's Vietnam policy. Communism was seen as a menace to peace and freedom throughout the world, and the United States was committed to stopping its spread. Many Americans clearly remembered the Allied victory at the close of World War II, only twenty years before. Surely, their country fought on the side of truth and justice. Certainly it could never be defeated.

When students at the University of California's Berkeley campus demonstrated against the war in

September 1965, few Americans took their actions seriously. With their long hair and ragged jeans, the Berkeley protesters seemed to be a tiny minority with strange, radical ideas.

As the war dragged on, however, more and more Americans raised difficult questions. Why was the United States interfering in a civil war halfway around the world when it had desperate problems of its own at home? Why did America back Ky and Thieu, the South Vietnamese leaders who had little support from their own people? Why didn't people realize that war was evil and find better ways of resolving their differences? The more people questioned the war, the more they began to protest.

Early in the war, most of the protesters were college students. Young men of college age were eligible for the military draft. Under the draft system, every man in the United States was required to register when he turned eighteen. For the first few years, deferments were available to married men and students, as well as to those with health problems or disabilities. Most men who did not have deferments were eventually called for military duty. Some young men refused to register. A few burned their draft cards or left the United States for Canada. Some sought out doctors who would grant them a medical excuse.

The draft system drew heavily on young men from poor families who could not get deferment by staying in school. About 28 percent of the troops who served in Vietnam were African American, although African

As a sign of protest, young men burn their draft cards.

Americans comprised only 10 percent of the U.S. population. Most of the draft resisters were white and middle-class. They were people who had known many advantages in life and felt that their voices could have an impact on the decisionmakers in Washington.

Month by month the Pentagon called for more troops to fight the war, and the grim list of American casualties grew steadily longer. By December 1967, five hundred thousand Americans were serving in Vietnam. Some nine thousand had died in that year alone. From plush suburbs to Appalachian mining towns and urban slums, more and more families received the dreaded news. Then the corpse of a son or a husband returned in a flag-draped coffin, and there were words about the honor of dying for one's country. More and more people began to ask why.

The War of Words

Gradually the peace movement widened. Newspapers and national magazines printed heartbreaking stories of bombed villages and children with hideous wounds. One by one, Congressmen withdrew their support for the president's Vietnam policy and demanded that the United States withdraw from the conflict. On November 15, 1969, two hundred fifty thousand protesters marched in Washington, D.C., to show how they felt about the war. The marchers represented every sector of society—young and old, men and women, people of every race. They all cherished the same hope, that soon the death and destruction would come to an end.

Thousands of antiwar protesters from across the nation rally in Washington, D.C., in October 1967.

Antiwar feeling was by no means universal in the United States. Many Americans felt that the U.S. could win the war if it would only heighten its efforts. They considered the protesters unpatriotic, and some accused them of being Communist sympathizers. One popular bumper sticker proclaimed, "AMERICA: LOVE IT OR LEAVE IT." Another showed an American flag with the caption, "THESE COLORS DON'T RUN."

People came to identify themselves and one another as pro-war hawks or antiwar doves. Friendships shattered over differences of opinion about the war. Fathers disowned sons who dodged the draft. Yet while debates raged over dinner tables, in classrooms, and in the halls of Congress, bombs fell, mines exploded, and the death toll climbed ever higher.

A Nation of Refugees

On a January morning in 1967, the people of Ben Suc, in Duong Binh Province north of Saigon, woke to the roar of helicopters. The 2nd Brigade of the 173rd Army Airborne Division had launched Operation Cedar Falls, a surprise attack on Vietcong in Ben Suc and neighboring villages. With the help of a Vietnamese interpreter, American soldiers spent the morning questioning everyone in the village. In some cases, people were identified as Vietcong simply because they wore "black pajamas" like Ho Chi Minh and his peasant army. However, these loose black trousers were the traditional costume of country people in many parts of Vietnam. All Vietcong suspects were killed or taken prisoner. The rest of the villagers—mostly women, children, and old men—were loaded into trucks and driven to a hastily built refugee camp. When everyone had been evacuated, the village of Ben Suc was leveled with bombs in the hope that no Vietcong would ever hide there again.

The war wrought havoc in the lives of millions of civilians in North and South Vietnam. The Tet Offensive alone uprooted as many as one million people. Torn from their homes, their families killed or scattered, the refugees huddled in barbed-wire enclosures or drifted onto the streets of Saigon and Da Nang. Boys became thieves, and girls turned to prostitution to survive. Old people and ragged orphans begged for food or coins. The Vietnamese called these armies of homeless people *bui doi*—dust of life.

In South Vietnam, most fighting occurred in the villages, where the Vietcong and the government forces struggled for the loyalty of the people. Communist cadres threatened anyone who favored the South Vietnamese government, and the Americans and the ARVN attacked all those suspected of Communist leanings. It was dangerous to take either side, but neutrality was impossible.

The Vietcong encouraged all the people in a village to participate in the war effort. Children as young as twelve spied on government loyalists or warned visitors of land mines in the fields. No one's position was secure. A neighbor's accusation or a relative's indiscreet remark was enough to brand one an enemy. "If the Republicans [the ARVN] were like elephants trampling our village,

Carrying the few possessions they can salvage, terrified women and children flee the fighting in a South Vietnamese village.

the Vietcong were like snakes who came at us in the night," one South Vietnamese woman reflected years later. "At least you could see an elephant coming and get out of its way."[1]

Most villagers dug bomb shelters beneath their thatched huts. When planes droned in the distance, the family crowded into its hole and waited for the terrible pounding of explosives. One woman, Xuan Quynh, wrote poetry while she sat in her shelter with her infant son.

What do you have for a childhood,
That you still smile in the bomb shelter?
There is the morning wind which comes to visit you.
There is the full moon which follows you.
The long river, the immense sea,
A round pond, the enemy's bomb smoke,
The evening star.[2]

The relentless bombing of North Vietnam devastated hundreds of villages, killing as many as one hundred thousand civilians. Besides the bombs and napalm, the North Vietnamese endured the anguish of separation from their loved ones. By 1967, some twenty thousand people streamed south from North Vietnam each month. Most of the men and women who trudged the Ho Chi Minh Trail did not return for years, if they came home at all. "I didn't receive a single letter from my husband after he went south," said a woman from a village near Hanoi. "I wrote to him often, but I don't know whether he ever got my letters. Then one day I

South Vietnamese women soldiers patrol the outskirts of a village to discourage a Vietcong attack.

was suddenly handed an official notice saying that he had been killed . . . . Sometimes I think that I am going out of my mind, as if my soul had departed from my body."[3]

Early in the war, the South Vietnamese government erected a thirteen-foot concrete statue of an ARVN soldier on the highway north of Saigon. The soldier sat resting, his rifle across his knees, his head bowed in weariness. Some people said that the statue walked at night. Others claimed it called out to warn of coming disaster. Many people told how it wept during the terrible days of the Tet Offensive. A symbol of Vietnam's agony through the long years of war, the statue was entitled *Sorrow*.

The Sick and the Wounded

More than one million American men and women served in Vietnam during the course of the war. Some fifty-eight thousand Americans lost their lives. Thousands more were permanently disabled by the enemy shells or mines, or accidentally, by "friendly fire." Exposure to chemicals such as Agent Orange, used to destroy the dense jungle foliage where the Vietcong could hide, resulted in a host of lasting physical and psychological problems.

If a soldier was wounded, his squad leader immediately radioed for a Med-Evac (medical evacuation) helicopter. If all went smoothly, he was airlifted out of the jungle within twenty minutes and flown to the nearest field hospital. There he was examined in the triage room to determine the extent of his injuries. The triage system dated back to the First World War. Emergency patients were classified into three groups—those who could benefit from immediate care, those who could afford to wait for treatment, and those who were beyond hope.

Conditions in Vietnam's field hospitals were a shock to doctors and nurses used to the antiseptic facilities of the United States. Worst of all was the horror of seeing so many young men with ghastly injuries. Linda van Devanter, an army nurse, remembered her first day on duty at a hospital near Pleiku: "I saw young boys with their arms and legs blown off, some with their guts hanging out, and others with 'ordinary' gunshot wounds."[4] Her first patient was a boy who had been wounded by shrapnel, fragments from an exploding shell. "When a soldier got a frag wound, he would usually have little holes all over his body where the fragments had broken the skin. Our job, after we stopped the bleeding, was to remove the fragments and cut away any dead skin. . . . [The doctor] called it 'making big holes out of little holes.' "[5]

Land mines and ambushes were only some of the perils of jungle patrols. Mosquitoes carried deadly malaria and other diseases. Parasites infested food and drinking water. Many men developed oozing ulcers on their feet and legs from the constant dampness. Even life at base camp claimed its victims. By 1970 as many as one in three servicemen used heroin or other drugs, and alcoholism was widespread. There were fights between soldiers or between Americans and Vietnamese civilians.

The fighting leaves a 3-year-old boy wounded, homeless, and fatherless.

In addition to treating sick and wounded soldiers, U.S. medical teams worked among the Vietnamese people. Providing medical care to the villagers was a crucial feature in America's pacification program. Through the pacification program, the United States opened clinics and schools in an effort to win the people's loyalty. Doctors and nurses dispensed antibiotics, aspirins, and even bars of soap. Most of the villagers had never seen such marvels before and found them strange and magical.

The North Vietnamese and the Vietcong operated a series of field hospitals along the Ho Chi Minh Trail in Laos and Cambodia. In Vietnam, many of their medical facilities were literally underground. Deep below the earth's surface in a labyrinth of caves and tunnels, they were relatively safe from bombs. Doctors and nurses cleaned and bandaged wounds by the light of kerosene lamps. Under seemingly impossible conditions, they did their best to save lives.

Prisoners of War

The smoke had barely cleared in the Gulf of Tonkin on August 5, 1964, when Navy Lieutenant J.G. Everett Alvarez set out in an A-4 Skyhawk fighter plane for North Vietnam. After a bombing raid on Hong Dai Harbor, Alvarez turned and headed back to the carrier U.S.S. *Constellation.* Suddenly, antiaircraft fire hit his plane and he parachuted safely into the sea. Excited fishermen hauled him into their sampan and turned him over to North Vietnamese authorities. Lt. Alvarez was the first of hundreds of prisoners of war (POWs) taken

A medic treats an American lieutenant, his leg burned by a Vietcong
booby trap.

by the North Vietnamese. He spent a record eight and one-half years in captivity, more time than any other American prisoner of any other war.

Like Alvarez, most of the POWs were Navy or Air Force pilots or air crew members shot down on bombing raids over North Vietnam. The majority were officers captured during the years of heavy bombing between 1965 and 1968 or during renewed bombing attacks which occurred in 1972. A few other military and civilian prisoners were taken in South Vietnam and in Laos.

For the most part, American POWs in North Vietnam were held in or around Hanoi. With an unflagging sense of humor, the POWs gave their prisons a variety of nicknames—the Plantation, the Zoo, Skid Row, and the Rock Pile. One remote prison near the Chinese border was called Dogpatch, after the backwoods town in the "Little Abner" comic strip. The main prison, Hoa Loh (the Hanoi Hilton), had been built by the French. It was an impregnable fortress, its twenty-foot walls topped with broken glass and electrified wire, guard towers glaring from each corner.

Under the internationally approved Code of Conduct for prisoners, the POWs were required to reveal only their name, rank, military serial number, and date of birth. But their captors were eager to gain vital information about American plans and technology. They also hoped to grind down the prisoners' loyalty to the United States to force them to make anti-American, pro-Communist statements which could be used as propaganda. If they refused to cooperate, prisoners were placed in solitary confinement or subjected to physical torture.

In an interview a few weeks after his release in 1973, Air Force Major Konrad W. Trautman described a common torture method.

> Remember when you were a little boy . . . and someone grabs your hand and just twists your arm up to your back and says, 'Say uncle!' . . . Well, imagine this with both arms tied tight together, elbow to elbow, wrist to wrist, and then, using the leverage of his feet planted between your shoulder blades, with both hands he pulls with all his might until your arms are up and back over your head, forcing your head down and between your feet, where your legs are between iron bars. . . . I would rather spend six months in solitary confinement than go through one fifteen-minute rope session.[6]

The prisoners endured their ordeal with extraordinary fortitude. They kept their sanity in solitary confinement by reciting poetry, working complex mathematical problems, and remembering every detail about life outside with their friends and families. One prisoner spent an entire year building a house in his head. In his imagination he sawed every board, hammered each nail, measured every angle, and set the bricks into place one by one.

More than anything else, the prisoners drew strength from one another. When they were forbidden to converse, they tapped out coded messages on their cell walls

A Vietnamese farmer is forced to flee from his home.

or slipped each other notes printed on toilet paper. They sustained each other through pain, fear, and aching homesickness. Men from vastly different backgrounds lived together for years, sharing every moment of the day, helping each other to survive. "You learned tolerance. You learn a lot of tolerance," reflected one former prisoner. "We learned to love each other."[7]

In April 1973, Hanoi officials released 564 military and 23 civilian prisoners of war. But more than one thousand Americans remained missing in action. Many people in the United States believed that some of these MIAs were still held in North Vietnamese prisons or that they were being used as slave laborers. Families and friends of the MIAs pressured the U.S. government to demand their return. Into the 1990s, rumors continued to surface that Americans were alive in Vietnam. But by that time most authorities were convinced that all of the MIAs were killed during the war.

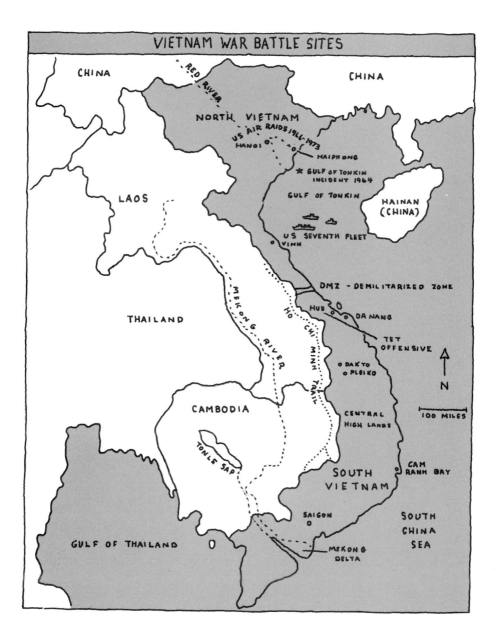

VIETNAM WAR BATTLE SITES

CHINA

CHINA

RED RIVER

NORTH VIETNAM

US AIR RAIDS 1966-1973

HANOI ○   ○   HAIPHONG

★ GULF OF TONKIN
INCIDENT 1964

GULF OF TONKIN

HAINAN
(CHINA)

LAOS

US SEVENTH FLEET
○ VINH

THAILAND

MEKONG RIVER

HO CHI MINH TRAIL

DMZ - DEMILITARIZED ZONE

HUE ○   ○
DA NANG

TET
OFFENSIVE

○ DAK TO
○ PLEIKU

↑
N

100 MILES

CAMBODIA

CENTRAL
HIGH LANDS

TON LE SAP

CAM
RANH BAY

SOUTH
VIETNAM

SAIGON
○

SOUTH
CHINA
SEA

GULF OF THAILAND

○

MEKONG
DELTA

If when the chips are down, the world's most powerful nation . . . acts like a pitiful, helpless giant, the forces of totalitarianism and anarchy will threaten free nations and free institutions throughout the world.
> —President Richard M. Nixon, in a televised speech, April 30, 1970.

6 The Road to Peace

 In Vietnam, white is the traditional color of mourning. On September 3, 1969, people all over North Vietnam dressed in white to mourn the death of their longtime leader, Ho Chi Minh. Uncle Ho, at the age of 79, was gone, but the war raged unabated. Soldiers and ammunition, medicine and guns poured into South Vietnam along the Ho Chi Minh Trail.

The Widening War
In the early years of the war, the parts of the trail which wound through the countries of Laos and Cambodia were off limits to American bombers. The American public saw invasion of these countries as expansion of the war and a growing threat to world peace. There was always the danger that the Soviet Union and China

might step from behind the scenes and confront the United States head on. Such a direct confrontation could possibly spiral into nuclear war.

A week after President Nixon took office, he discussed the situation in Vietnam with General Creighton Abrams. Abrams replaced Westmoreland as commander of American operations in Vietnam in July 1968. Convinced that the United States must shift its tactics in order to win the war, Abrams urged Nixon to bomb the North Vietnamese supply route through Cambodia. On March 17, 1969, the United States launched its first bombing assault on the Cambodian section of the Ho Chi Minh Trail. Cambodia's leader, Prince Sihanouk, gave his tacit permission for the anti-Communist attacks. But Nixon kept the bombings secret from the American public. For the next fourteen months the raids continued, without the knowledge of Congress or the American people. Even many top White House officials remained unaware of the president's actions.

By the end of 1968, the fighting in Vietnam had cost thirty thousand American lives. The Nixon administration was under increasing pressure to find a way out of the war. In March 1969, Defense Secretary Melvin Laird stated a new policy—the "Vietnamization" of the conflict. The South Vietnamese would take greater responsibility for the war effort, and American forces would gradually be withdrawn. In June, Nixon announced that twenty-five thousand American troops would be coming home.

In May 1969, the war swept into living-rooms across

Reconnaissance photographs reveal trucks from North Vietnam moving along the Ho Chi Minh Trail.

America with renewed horror. Some twenty-eight hundred American troops under Lieutenant Colonel Weldon Honeycutt launched a massive assault on the North Vietnamese on a mountain near the Laotian border. On military maps, the mountain was designated Hill 837. So many men were cut to pieces by bombs and artillery that it earned the nickname Hamburger Hill. Then, the day after the North Vietnamese were finally driven off the mountain, the Americans received inexplicable orders to withdraw. Within a month, Hill 837 was in Communist hands once more.

Another horror story from Vietnam broke in November when American reporters learned of an incident which had occurred more than a year before. On March 16, 1968, an army platoon under Lieutenant William Calley began a routine search-and-destroy mission at the South Vietnamese village of My Lai. Somehow the search for Vietcong suspects ended in a spree of senseless violence. The soldiers dashed from hut to hut, murdering everyone they found. According to some estimates, as many as four hundred people died before the bloodbath came to an end. The brutality shocked even the most war-hardened Americans. Something had gone dreadfully wrong. The United States was fighting to save the South Vietnamese, while American soldiers destroyed them day by day.

Meanwhile, as Nixon talked about troop withdrawals from Vietnam, the secret bombing strikes over Cambodia continued. Prince Sihanouk's popularity quickly eroded. North Vietnamese Communists began to infiltrate

President Richard M. Nixon and General Creighton Abrams discuss the war in Vietnam. Nixon ordered the secret bombing of the Ho Chi Minh Trail.

Cambodia, triggering a bloody civil war. Sihanouk was deposed early in 1970, and Nixon decided to support his successor, the anti-Communist General Lon Nol.

On April 30, Nixon appeared on nationwide television and announced his decision to send arms, advisers, and ground troops into Cambodia. The United States would now be supporting the besieged government in Phnom Pehn, Cambodia, as well as the struggling regime of Thieu in Saigon, Vietnam.

Outrage resounded from college campuses all the way to the top levels of government. Secretary of the Interior Walter Hickel condemned Nixon's policy and was dismissed from office. More than two hundred state department officials signed a petition of protest. Students all over the country raised an outcry against the betrayal of Nixon's promise of peace.

At Kent State University in northern Ohio, student protesters set fire to the campus Reserve Officers Training Corps (ROTC) building. Ohio Governor James Rhodes called in the National Guard to quell the disorder. Though the demonstrators were unarmed, the National Guard opened fire on the crowd. Nine students were wounded, and four were killed. A week later, police in armored tanks killed two students and wounded several more at Jackson State College in Mississippi.

The deaths at Kent State and Jackson State sent shock waves across the already deeply troubled nation. At more than four hundred colleges and universities, classes were suspended and students took to the streets in massive rallies. Some one hundred thousand demonstrators marched on Washington and encircled the White House.

Throughout these turbulent weeks, the Nixon administration appeared almost indifferent. There was no heartfelt public apology for the campus shootings. Instead, Nixon's press secretary, Ron Ziegler, stated, "When dissent turns to violence, it invites tragedy."

Desperate Measures

Despite the protests and the violence, President Nixon insisted that he had the support of America's silent majority. He remained firmly convinced that the United States must not lose the respect of the world by withdrawing from Vietnam.

In 1971, U.S. and ARVN forces stepped up bombing missions over parts of the Mekong Delta where the Vietcong were thought to hide. Navy Pilot Kit Lavell flew a twin-engine turbo prop plane similar to aircraft which had been used during World War II. Though it was small and could not gain much altitude, it was easy to maneuver and permitted highly accurate strikes. "We literally flew at treetop level," Lavell recalled. "We flew around the clock seven days a week, night and day without stop, loaded with about three thousand pounds of forward firing ordnance primarily. Sixty percent of my missions were at night, mostly in bad weather . . . We literally flew seat of the pants and had to fly underneath the clouds. . . . On more than eighty percent of the missions we took fire."[1]

On February 8, 1971, thirty thousand South Vietnamese

ground troops invaded Laos and pressed toward the Communist stronghold of Tchepone on the Ho Chi Minh Trail. Called Operation Lam Son 719, the campaign was part of the Vietnamization plan—the South Vietnamese were to function without the help of American advisers. The assault was designed too hastily, and the ARVN forces were inadequate and poorly armed. The South Vietnamese clashed with the North Vietnamese Army (NVA) several miles before their destination. In a month of fierce, bloody fighting, the ARVN suffered more than three thousand casualties.

The South Vietnamese troops finally broke into frantic retreat, flinging down their rifles and backpacks, fleeing for their lives. "They shelled us first, and then came the tanks," one private recalled later. "The whole brigade ran down the hill like ants. We jumped on each other to get out of that place. No man had time to look for his commanding officer. It was quick! quick! quick! or we would die. Oh God! Now I know for sure that I am really alive!"[2] Some desperate soldiers clung to the skids of rescue helicopters that were packed to capacity. Slashed by the wind, they hung on until their icy fingers slipped and they plunged from the sky.

The debacle of Lam Son 719 demoralized the ARVN. The U.S. forces in Vietnam had also reached a low point in morale. Some men simply refused to obey orders. A few even turned on their officers, "fragging" them with hand grenades—weapons that left no fingerprints. To make the situation even worse, growing

In a village fifteen miles west of Da Nang, a Vietcong suspect is led away for questioning by a U.S. Marine.

tension between white and black troops sometimes erupted into violence. As the soldiers grew more discouraged, they turned increasingly to drugs. One brigade officer commented, "When a man is in Vietnam, he is sure that no matter where he is, who he is with, or who he is talking to, there are probably drugs within twenty-five feet of him."[3]

In the spring of 1971, a former Pentagon bureaucrat named Daniel Ellsberg presented a series of military documents to the *New York Times*. The documents—an extensive collection of letters, memos, and cables exchanged between top military and government leaders—disclosed America's gradual commitment to the war in Vietnam. They revealed how that commitment was hidden from the public until the middle of the Johnson administration. They also showed an appalling lack of concern for the human cost of the fighting. The *New York Times* published the first of the "Pentagon Papers" on June 13, 1971.

President Nixon was incensed when the Pentagon Papers hit the newsstands. He ordered that their publication should halt at once, as it posed a threat to national security. Within two weeks, the U.S. Supreme Court ruled that Nixon's order violated the right to freedom of the press under the constitution. "Paramount among the responsibilities of a free press is the duty to prevent any part of the government from deceiving the people and sending them off to distant lands to die of foreign fevers and foreign shot and shell," wrote Justice Hugo L. Black. ". . . In revealing the workings of government that led to

the Vietnam War, the newspapers nobly did precisely what the founders hoped and trusted they would do."[4]

The Pentagon Papers incident was the final blow to Nixon's sense of power and control. He organized a team of top-level White House staff members to hunt out the enemies who seemed to hound him on all sides. These staffers were nicknamed the Plumbers because they were ordered to plug up information leaks to the press. A year after the Pentagon Papers appeared, a night watchman discovered some of the Plumbers as they broke into Democratic campaign headquarters at Washington's Watergate Hotel complex. The ensuing furor over the Watergate scandal unraveled Nixon's political career and finally forced him to resign from office in August 1974.

The Easter Offensive

Early in 1972, North Vietnamese forces under General Giap amassed along the 17th parallel in preparation for a major offensive. The assault began on March 30—Good Friday on the Christian calendar. With armored tanks, heavy artillery, and one hundred twenty-five thousand troops, the NVA thundered over the border into South Vietnam.

The Easter Offensive, as it came to be known, was a bold attempt to overrun all of South Vietnam and bring the war to a close. As they had in the Tet Offensive, the Communists struck many targets at once. While troops from the north attacked the cities of Quang Tri and Hue, more forces surged in from Cambodia to strike towns around Saigon. Quang Tri fell quickly, but the able leadership of ARVN Major General Ngo Quang Truong saved Hue from capture. Colonel Ly Tong Ba and his ARVN 23rd Infantry Division performed heroically at the city of Kontum. With the help of American B-52 bombers, they drove back the enemy after weeks of bloody fighting. Further south, the Communists threatened the city of Anh Loc near Saigon but were thwarted by Major General James "Holly" Hollingsworth, a brash Texan serving as senior adviser to the Third ARVN Corps. By the end of September, the Communists were forced to give up Quang Tri and their other gains in South Vietnam. In the course of the Easter Offensive, the NVA suffered nearly one hundred thousand casualties.

President Nixon responded to the Easter Offensive by authorizing renewed bombing raids on North Vietnam. The north had not been bombed since 1968. The new raids included strikes on Hanoi and Haiphong, which President Johnson had placed off limits due to their heavy civilian populations. Furthermore, Nixon called for the mining of Haiphong Harbor, North Vietnam's major shipping center. Polls indicated that Nixon's actions had strong, though silent, support throughout the nation. But antiwar protesters and even many more moderate voices cried out in horror. Many Soviet vessels were anchored at Haiphong. Their destruction could be the spark to set off a war with Russia. Yet Nixon was convinced there could be no honorable peace unless the United States took decisive action.

Cease Fire

In May 1968, delegates from South Vietnam, North Vietnam, the Vietcong, and the United States met in Paris and opened the first negotiations for peace. Almost at once, the talks bogged down in a mire of detail. The delegates argued over virtually everything—even the shape of the bargaining table.

In 1969, President Nixon appointed Henry A. Kissinger to serve as his National Security Adviser. Kissinger was born in Germany and immigrated to the United States as a teenager to escape anti-Jewish persecution under the Nazis. At Harvard University he became a noted expert on foreign affairs. During the Nixon Administration, Kissinger spearheaded the difficult, endlessly frustrating talks which the world hoped would end the war in Vietnam.

After nearly a year of fruitless discussions, Kissinger recognized that the Paris talks were futile. While the wrangling continued among the delegates, he entered into secret negotiations with a key North Vietnamese official, Le Duc Tho. Beginning on February 20, 1971, they met regularly in a run-down neighborhood on the outskirts of Paris. Though they avoided much of the squabbling that disrupted the larger meetings, the negotiating process remained painfully slow.

Finally, after the massive bombing strikes late in 1972, the delegates came to a definite agreement. The treaty between the United States, North Vietnam, and South Vietnam was signed at last on January 27, 1973. It called for an immediate cease-fire between American and North Vietnamese forces. Prisoners would be exchanged, and the United States would withdraw its military presence from Vietnam. The treaty did not, however, stipulate a cease-fire between North Vietnam and South Vietnam. Nevertheless, it did call for the two Vietnams to form a council of reconciliation which should work toward the eventual reunification of the country. For their efforts to build the peace accord, Kissinger and Le Duc Tho were awarded the Nobel Peace Prize in 1973.

By the time the peace agreement was signed, only a few thousand American combat troops were left in Vietnam. The last troops departed on March 29, 1973 and North Vietnam completed the release of its American prisoners of war on April 1. At last, America had reached the end of its longest war.

The United States had poured an estimated 150 billion dollars into the Vietnam conflict. Some fifty-eight thousand Americans had lost their lives, and perhaps fifteen hundred or more were missing in action. For the first time in its history of nearly two hundred years, America tasted defeat.

The End of a Long, Sad War

The cease-fire agreement sparked no joyful celebrations in South Vietnam. Sporadic fighting continued as though nothing had changed. President Thieu publicly declared that the cease-fire was not a peace agreement; it simply meant that the Americans were abandoning South Vietnam to its fate.

On January 27, 1973, Henry Kissinger signs the treaty which ends American involvement in the Vietnam War.

The heavy bombing of 1972 had destroyed roads, railways, and bridges in North Vietnam. For nearly two years after the cease-fire agreement was signed, the government in Hanoi worked to rebuild the country. At the same time, quietly and methodically, it prepared for the final onslaught against South Vietnam.

The last stage of the war began in January 1975, when an NVA force of three hundred thousand men rolled across the Cambodian border and overran Phuoc Lon Province north of Saigon. The invasion effectively cut South Vietnam in two, separating the ARVN forces in Saigon from those in the Central Highlands to the north. President Thieu ordered the ARVN troops in Hue and Pleiku to march south and defend the capital. In the days that followed, the orderly march turned into a frantic retreat as the ARVN fled before savage Communist pursuers. Thousands of panic-stricken civilians snatched up their meager possessions and joined the flight to the south. Countless people died of starvation or were killed by the enemy on the journey, which was remembered as the Convoy of Tears.

Late in March, the cities of Hue and Da Nang fell to the Communists. Under General Van Tien Dung, the North Vietnamese prepared to storm Saigon. They called this final assault the Ho Chi Minh Campaign.

The South Vietnamese army made its final stand at the town of Xuan Loc on the road to Saigon. Though hopelessly outnumbered, the ARVN troops held Xuan Loc for twelve tortured days. Xuan Loc fell at last on April 21, and President Thieu resigned.

Vietnamese refugees crowd aboard the carrier U.S.S. *Midway* in April, 1975, to escape Communist takeover.

In desperation, thousands of South Vietnamese fled the country before the Communist advance. Some escaped on the last ARVN Air Force planes which lifted off from Tan Son Nhut Airfield. Others crowded onto barges and headed down the Saigon River to waiting American rescue ships. "The situation was pitiful, unbelievable and heart-rending," the captain of one ship recalled. "At [8 P.M.] we had to stop, with an estimated 10,000 refugees on board, and just no room for any others. Seventy or eighty boats were still alongside us and pleading with us please to take them. We had to cut boats loose in order to get away. . . . We did our best, and yet it seemed so inadequate."[5]

Back in Washington, Congress refused to authorize any more money for the collapsing South Vietnamese government. But it did vote to send Marines and Army troops to evacuate the last American civilians from Saigon. On April 30, three Marine helicopter squadrons and ten Air Force helicopters zoomed in over the beleaguered city. Landing on parking lots, tennis courts, and the roofs of buildings, they swept the last Americans out of the maelstrom to safety. As an epilogue to America's first defeat, the Saigon Air Lift was carried out with decision and heroism.

On May 1, Le Duc Tho entered Saigon with the first NVA ground troops. The North Vietnamese flag rose over the Presidential Palace, and Saigon was given a new name. From that day forward, it would be known as Ho Chi Minh City. After thirty years of fighting, Vietnam was one nation, independent and united at last.

Nobody is more antiwar than a person who has been to war.
—Lt. Col. H. Norman Schwarzkopf, in an interview in 1974.[1]

7 The Legacy of War

Every day, thousands of Americans visit a V-shaped monument of glossy black granite which stands on the Capitol Mall in Washington, D.C. Some search among the inscriptions carved in the stone. Many stand and weep. Others simply gaze in silence at the wall, covered with the names of the U.S. men and women who died in Vietnam between 1959 and 1975.

The Vietnam Veterans Memorial officially opened on November 11, 1982. Within the first five years, it received 20 million visitors. In its stark simplicity, the wall came to symbolize America's struggle to heal the wounds left by the long and bitter war.

Most Vietnam veterans eventually adjusted to civilian life. But thousands experienced severe depression and other symptoms which doctors called post-traumatic stress syndrome. Others developed a strange assortment of medical problems. Many of their difficulties were traced to exposure to Agent Orange, a chemical which was used to kill dense jungle foliage.

The veterans of most previous American wars returned as heroes. But the soldiers who came home from Vietnam received no heroes' welcome. Remembering stories of My Lai and other atrocities, some people saw these soldiers as unbalanced, or as potential criminals. Others regarded the veterans as the unfortunate victims of America's terrible mistake. Yet as the years passed, more and more Americans came to respect them as survivors of an extraordinary ordeal. In books, plays, and films, the nation sought to understand and learn from the Vietnam experience.

The War in Vietnam left America with much to ponder about its role in the modern world. Could the United States be expected to intervene in far-flung countries whenever democracy was threatened? Was the need to save face with the international community worth the loss of thousands of lives? Perhaps America needed to learn a new sense of humility and a greater respect for the peoples of other nations. In the ensuing decades, whenever policymakers considered sending American troops to fight in some troubled land overseas, voices rose in protest, crying, "No more Vietnams!"

The Vietnam War had a profound impact upon American life and thought. Yet in the end, most Americans

Each year thousands of visitors leave cherished keepsakes in remembrance at the Vietnam Veterans War Memorial.

could turn away and get on with their lives. The Vietnamese lived with the devastation of the war all around them. Everywhere fields and forests were pitted with craters from bombs and artillery shells. Nearly every family had lost husbands or sons to the fighting. Millions of refugees wandered the land, uprooted from homes where they had lived for countless generations. Old resentments festered, and old hatreds ran deep.

The Communists had been masters at waging war. But the task of uniting the shattered nation proved nearly overwhelming. Some former North Vietnamese found themselves looking back at the war years almost with nostalgia. "Since the end of the war, without the bombs dropping, we have lost much of [our] fervor," commented Tan Phat Tung, who once served as a physician with the NVA. "We complain about food and housing shortages, complaints never heard during the war, when nobody cared what they ate or how they slept. The change is strange and paradoxical."[2]

The Vietnamese and American people will bear the scars of the Vietnam War for generations to come. The Vietnam Veterans Memorial was created to help heal the emotional and spiritual wounds which the war left as its legacy. It was this healing process which art student Maya Ying Lin envisioned when she designed the monument. "When you leave the memorial, you have to walk back up into the light. You must choose to do it, to go beyond. To me it is very much a journey. You have to walk out and leave it in the end."[3]

Chronology

March 13–May 7, 1954—Vietminh under Vo Nguyen Giap defeat the French at Dien Bien Phu.

May 8, 1954—Beginning of Indochina discussion at the Geneva Conference. Final agreement divides Vietnam along the 17th parallel into Communist-controlled North and democratic South.

1955—U.S. begins sending money to aid South Vietnam. President Eisenhower agrees to help train South Vietnamese Army.

May, 1959—North Vietnamese begin to infiltrate South Vietnam, moving men and supplies along the Ho Chi Minh Trail.

July 8, 1959—Two Americans are killed by Communists at Bien Hoa, the first Americans to die in the Vietnam conflict.

1960—Hanoi leaders form the National Liberation Front, which South Vietnamese President Ngo Dinh Diem calls the Vietcong.

1962—South Vietnamese government promotes strategic hamlets program. Number of American advisers in Vietnam increases from 700 to 12,000.

January 2, 1963—Vietcong defeat Army of the Republic of Vietnam (ARVN) in the Battle of Ap Bac.

May 8, 1963—South Vietnamese troops fire on crowd of Buddhists at festival in Hue.

November 1, 1963—With the tacit approval of the U.S., South Vietnamese generals overthrow and murder Diem and his brother Nhu.

August 1, 1964—North Vietnamese patrolboats attack the U.S. destroyer *Maddox* in the Gulf of Tonkin.

August 5, 1964—American forces bomb North Vietnam.

August 7, 1964—Congress passes the Gulf of Tonkin Resolution, giving the President the right to handle the Vietnam conflict as he sees fit.

January–February, 1965—Vietcong launch a series of attacks against American bases in South Vietnam.

February 24, 1965—The United States begins Operation Rolling Thunder, the sustained bombing of North Vietnam.

March 8, 1965—Two Marine battalions land at Da Nang, the first American ground troops to arrive in Vietnam.

June 1, 1965 Air Vice Marshal Nguyen Cao Ky heads South Vietnamese government, ending nearly two years of unrest.

1966—American forces continue bombing of North Vietnam and carry on search–and–destroy missions in the south.

September, 1967—General William Westmoreland orders fortification of Khe Sanh.

December, 1967—Communists hold Americans and South Vietnamese at Khe Sanh under siege.

January 31, 1968—Tet Offensive begins with scattered Communist attacks throughout South Vietnam.

February, 1968—General Creighton Abrams replaces Westmoreland as commander of American operations in Vietnam.

March 25, 1968—President Lyndon Johnson meets with top advisers, who recommend against further escalation of the war.

March 31, 1968—Johnson announces that he will not seek re–election.

May, 1968—Peace negotiations begin in Paris.

August, 1968—Johnson halts American bombing of North Vietnam.

March 18, 1969—President Nixon begins secret bombing strikes on the Ho Chi Minh Trail in Cambodia.

November 15, 1969—Massive antiwar demonstrations are held in Washington and cities throughout the country.

February 20, 1970—National Security Adviser Henry Kissinger begins secret peace talks with North Vietnamese delegate Le Duc Thoh in Paris.

April 30, 1970—President Nixon announces American and South Vietnamese invasion of Cambodia.

May 4, 1970—Four student demonstrators are killed by the National Guard at Kent State University.

February, 1971—ARVN defeated in thrust toward Tchepone in Laos.

June 13, 1971—The *New York Times* begins publishing the Pentagon Papers.

March 31, 1972—North Vietnam launches the Easter Offensive across the 17th parallel.

April 15, 1972—President Nixon authorizes renewed bombing of North Vietnam.

January 27, 1973—Cease–fire agreement between the U.S., North Vietnam, and South Vietnam is signed in Paris.

March 29, 1973—The last American troops leave Vietnam.

April 29, 1975—Saigon Air Lift evacuates last American civilians from Vietnam.

April 30, 1975—North Vietnamese Army captures Saigon, renaming it Ho Chi Minh City. Vietnam is united under one government.

Notes by Chapter

Chapter 1

1. Karnow, Stanley. *Vietnam: a History*. New York: Viking, 1983, p. 281.

2. Boettcher, Thomas B. *Vietnam: The Valor and the Sorrow, from the Home Front to the Front Lines in Words and Pictures*. Boston: Little Brown, 1985, p. 192.

3. Karnow, Stanley. p. 374.

Chapter 2

1. Karnow, Stanley. *Vietnam: a History*. New York: Viking, 1983, p. 86.

2. *Ibid.*, p. 135.

3. Davidson, Philip A. *Vietnam at War: 1946-1975*. Novato, CA: Presidio Press, 1988, p. 227.

4. *Ibid.*, p. 256-257.

Chapter 3

1. Sully, Francois and Marjorie Weiner Normand. *We the Vietnamese: Voices from Vietnam*. New York: Praeger, 1971, p. 255.

2. Emerson, Gloria. *Winners and Losers: Battles, Retreats, Gains, Losses, and Ruins from a Long War*. New York: Random House, 1976, p. 74.

3. Karnow, Stanley. *Vietnam: a History*. New York: Viking, 1983, p. 281.

4. Boettcher, Thomas B. *Vietnam: The Valor and the Sorrow, from the Home Front to the Front Lines in Words and Pictures.* Boston: Little Brown, 1985, p. 192.

5. Karnow, Stanley. p. 289.

6. *Ibid.,* p. 322.

7. *Ibid.,* p. 374.

Chapter 4

1. Karnow, Stanley. *Vietnam, a History.* New York: Viking, 1983, p. 140.

2. *Ibid.,* p. 455.

3. Terry, Wallace, ed. *Bloods: an Oral History of the Vietnam War by Black Veterans.* New York: Ballantine, 1984, p. 34.

4. Edelman, Bernard, ed. *Dear America: Letters Home from Vietnam.* New York: Pocket, 1985, p. 18.

5. Santoli, Al, ed. *Everything We Had: an Oral History of the Vietnam War by Thirty-three Soldiers Who Fought It.* New York: Random House, 1981, p. 153.

6. Terry, Wallace. p. 16.

7. Herring, George C. *America's Longest War: the United States in Vietnam, 1950-1975.* New York: John Wiley, 1979, p. 187.

8. *Ibid.,* p. 183.

9. Karnow, Stanley. p. 396.

Chapter 5

1. Hayslip, Le Ly. *When Heaven and Earth Changed Places: a Vietnamese Woman's Journey from War to Peace.* New York: Doubleday, 1989, p. 69.

2. van Devanter, Linda and Joan A. Furey. *Visions of War, Dreams of Peace: Writings of Women in the Vietnam War.* New York: Warner, 1991, p. 32.

3. Karnow, Stanley. *Vietnam: a History.* New York: Viking, 1983, p. 459.

4. van Devanter, Linda and Christopher Morgan. *Home before Morning: the Story of an Army Nurse in Vietnam.* New York, Toronto: Beaufort Books, 1983, p. 84.

5. *Ibid.,* p. 86.

6. Rowan, Stephen A. *They Wouldn't Let Us Die: the Prisoners of War Tell Their Story.* Middle Village, New York: Jonathan David Publishers, 1973, p. 45.

7. *Ibid.,* p. 153.

Chapter 6

1. Santoli, Al, ed. *Everything We Had: an Oral History of the Vietnam War by Thirty-three Americans Who Fought It.* New York: Random House, 1981, p. 114.

2. Emerson, Gloria. *Winners and Losers: Battles, Retreats, Gains, Losses, and Ruins from a Long War.* New York: Random House, 1976, p. 124.

3. Boettcher, Thomas B. *Vietnam: the Valor and the Sorrow, from the Home Front to the Front Lines in Words and Pictures.* Boston: Little Brown, 1985, p. 402.

4. Sheehan, Neil, Hendrick Smith, E. W. Kenworthy, and Fox Butterfield, ed. *The Pentagon Papers.* New York: Bantam, 1973, p. 1.

5. Isaacs, Arnold R. *Without Honor: Defeat in Vietnam and Cambodia.* Baltimore: John Hopkins University Press, 1983, p. 461-462.

Chapter 7

1. Bryan, C. D. D. *Friendly Fire.* New York: Putnam, 1976, p. 305.

2. Karnow, Stanley. *Vietnam: a History.* New York: Viking, 1983, p. 459.

3. Palmer, Laura. *Shrapnel from the Heart: Letters and Remembrances from the Vietnam Veterans Memorial.* New York: Vintage, 1987, p. XIX.

Further Reading

Fincher, E. B. *The Vietnam War.* New York: Franklin Watts, 1980.

Garland, Sherry. *Vietnam: Rebuilding a Nation.* New York: Dillon, 1990.

Hauptly, Denis. *In Vietnam.* New York: Atheneum, 1985.

Lawson, Don. *The War in Vietnam.* New York: Franklin Watts, 1981.

Nhuong, Nuynh Guang. *The Land I Lost: Adventures of a Boy in Vietnam.* New York: Harper, 1982.

Nickelson, Henry. *Vietnam.* San Diego: Lucent Books, 1989.

Willis, Charles. *The Tet Offensive.* Morristown, NJ: Silver Burdett, 1989.

Wright, David K. *Vietnam.* Chicago: Childrens Press, 1989.

Index

About the Author

Deborah Kent grew up in Little Falls, New Jersey. She received a B.A. from Oberlin College in Oberlin, Ohio, and a Master's Degree from Smith College School for Social Work. After four years as a social worker at the University Settlement House on New York City's Lower East Side, she decided to try her hand at writing. She moved to San Miguel de Allende, a Mexican town with a large community of writers and artists. Her first novel, *Belonging,* appeared in 1978.

Ms. Kent is the author of more than a dozen young-adult novels, as well as many nonfiction books for children. She lives in Chicago with her husband, children's-book author R. Conrad Stein, and their daughter Janna.